To the last 1/3 of all the Dads out there.

Promise kept.

I0149223

Dad Joke Books from T. J. Alex:

Roll-A-Joke Books:

Roll-A-Joke Dad Jokes: Vol. 1
Roll-A-Joke Dad Jokes: Vol. 2
Roll-A-Joke Dad Jokes: Vol. 3
Roll-A-Joke Dad Jokes: Vol. 4
Roll-A-Joke Dad Jokes: Vol. 5
Roll-A-Joke Dad Jokes: Vol. 6

601 Dad Joke Books:

601 Dad Jokes; or Puns of the Patriarchy: Vol. 1
601 Dad Jokes; or Puns of the Patriarchy: Vol. 2
601 Dad Jokes; or Puns of the Patriarchy: Vol. 3

Dad Joke Coloring Books (Coming Soon):

Dad Jokes: The Coloring Book: Vol. 1
Dad Jokes: The Coloring Book: Vol. 2
Dad Jokes: The Coloring Book: Vol. 3

If you like this book, please leave positive feedback on Amazon!

601 DAD JOKES

Volume 3

The most eye-rolling, groan-inducing, HEAD-SCRATCHING PUNS of ALL TIME!

T. J. Alex

XANDLAND XL PRESS

Published by Xandland Press

601 Dad Jokes: Volume 3 Copyright © T. J. Alex, 2025

ISBN-13: 978-1-95-492922-7

Printed in the United States

1 2 3 4 5 6 7 8 9 10 XP 30 29 28 27 26 25

If you shoot videos of your family enjoying this book and would like to be featured in social media, please email the footage to Xandland Press at info@xandland.com

To see what other Dad Joke books Xandland Press has to offer visit Xandland.com

About the Author:

T. J. Alex is the author of many Dad Joke books as well as a writer and editor on lots of other works. He also dabbles in screenplay writing.

He lives in Texas with his wife, three kids, and many, many, furry family members.

All of whom he tortures with the content you shall read here.

Introduction:

What makes the perfect Dad Joke? To me, it's two statements: a set-up and a payoff.

You'll see many joke books or social media pages that claim to tell Dad Jokes, but they will be full of questions with punch lines. For instance:

"Why did the scarecrow win an award? Because he was out standing in his field."

To me, that's not a Dad Joke. That's just a run-of-the-mill, ordinary joke. For it to be I Dad Joke, I'd rewrite it as:

"My scarecrow recently won an award.

He was out standing in his field."

See the difference? Two statements. Set-up. Payoff.

Probably 95% of the Dad Jokes in this book have been carefully chosen and re-written to make sure they not only meet my definition of a Dad Joke, but to also meet my high standards for humor and excellence.

Some people say I take this Dad Joke business too seriously, but I want the material I put out to be better than the rest.

Hopefully, you'll agree that this book, and the others I write, are outstanding in my field.

See what I did there?

A friend of mine fell into an upholstery machine.

He has since recovered.

I texted my girlfriend Ruth and told her it's over between us.

I'm Ruthless.

The doctor told me to eat lemon rinds for my cold.

It was a bitter peel to swallow.

There are a whole lot of people who are going nowhere in life.

People really need to stop asking me for directions.

I thought about trying on some shoes.

But my sole wasn't in it.

I jogged around the block today.

I couldn't get the ice cream truck to stop.

I love to tell towel jokes.

I have a dry sense of humor.

I got fired because a customer said I called her stupid.

That's no true. I asked her if she was stupid.

A friend said he didn't understand cloning.

That makes two of us.

Apparently, a non-binary person commited murder.

Because they slash them.

A friend who's getting married asked me how much a wedding band cost.

I said, "Well, it depends on the kind of music you want."

I forgot about the rehearsal for the street performance I'm learning to do.

Mime mistake.

A friend told me that he took off so fast, that his front tires came off the ground.

I said, "Wheelie?"

My wife asked me if she could have some peace and quiet while she cooks dinner.

So I took the batteries out of the smoke alarm.

Escalators are too slow.

Someone needs to invent an escasooner.

I bought some Right Guard deodorant the other day.

But I can't find Left Guard for my other armpit.

There was a long line to get my hair cut.

It was quite the barber-queue

My wife bought some odorless perfume.

That makes no scents.

I know a magician who works with dinosaurs.

He's got some T-rex up his sleeves.

I'm an expert in taking crushed dry leaves and heating them in water.

It's my special tea.

My son came to me and said, "Dad, are you embarrassed I'm your son?"

I looked him square in the eye and said, "Would you go over there? I don't want people to think we're together."

A friend of mine was bragging that he had a pen that could write underwater. I just laughed at him.

My pen can write a lot more words than that.

My friend Julie changed religions, and I can't say that I like it.

Christianlie is much harder to say.

I was going to start a support group for insomniacs.

If anyone's up for it.

I was late for work again.

Traffic was exactly the same as it has always been, and I wasn't expecting that.

I'm proud of my new whiteboard.

It's remarkable!

My astronaut friend was surprised at how long it is taking him to get readjusted after spending so much time in space.

He didn't realize the gravity of the situation.

I was going to get married in my flip flops.

But I got cold feet.

My wife is going on an all almond diet.

That's just nuts.

My daughter asked what you would call someone who had no body and nose.

Nobody knows.

The new toothpaste I bought is really bad.

It's ludaCrest.

Tea, coffee, and beer prices continue to rise.

Anger is brewing across the nation.

The other day when I was feeling depressed, my wife put her hand on my shoulder and said, "Earth."

It meant the world to me.

A lot of people call Santa's little helpers elves.

But I like to think of them as subordinate clauses.

I'm taking scuba diving lessons.

But I'm in over my head.

If you need proofreading services, then look no further.

From me, satisfaction is guaranteed or your monkey back.

My wife asked me if I'd seen the dog bowl.

I didn't know he could even lift a bowling ball.

I also try to tiptoe when I'm in a pharmacy.

I don't want to wake the sleeping pills.

The computer expert got in trouble for not declaring his income.

It was an all-cache business.

I told my son he shouldn't listen to losers.

Now he won't talk to me.

I guess you could say my first time on an elevator was an uplifting experience.

But the second time let me down.

I used to know a detective who solved cases accidentally.

His name was Sheer Luck Holmes.

I was astounded to learn the new statue wasn't made of stone.

I just took it for granite.

I've been doing crunches twice a day now.

Cap'n in the morning. Nestle in the afternoon.

Ireland's capital is the fastest growing city.

Every year, it's Dublin.

Our maintenance guy lost his legs on the job.

Now he's more of a handyman.

My wife told me to stop the dog from barking in the backseat.

So now he's barking in the front seat.

American children are kind.

But German children are kinder.

I'm gonna quit my job at the limo company.

After all this time, I've got nothing to chauffeur it.

It's no wonder actors are always told to break a leg.

Every play has a cast.

My wife is always putting things where I can't find it.

Yesterday she put my shoes on the shoe rack and my keys on the key hook.

There is a new store in town called Moderation.

They have everything there.

I recently took a poll.

100% of the people inside were mad when the tent collapsed.

A big shout-out to my grandmother.

That's the only way she'll hear me.

A slice of apple pie is $2.50 in Jamaica and $3.00 in the Bahamas.

They are the pie rates of the Caribbean.

I went out on a date last night with a girl who works at the zoo.

I think she's a keeper.

My son said that Ford invented the airplane.

That doesn't sound Wright.

I put all my money into buying sodas and storing it in my garage.

They are my liquid assets.

When one door closes, another one opens.

I'm gonna call the handyman to get that fixed.

The scientist thinks he can create a new way to freshen breath.

He's running experi-mints now.

The telegraph operator accidentally sent the same message twice.

He was re-morse-ful.

I know this lady who talks to her cat. She actually thinks the cat understands her.

My dog and I laugh about it all the time.

I wanted to tell a joke about restraining orders.

This is as close as I could get, though.

To start a zoo, you need two pandas, a grizzly, and three polar bears.

That's the bear minimum.

I've had to stop bringing my dog to the bar.

He can't control his licker.

Someone asked me if I know the symptoms are of my marriage phobia.

I can't say I do.

I lived in a haunted house, and the ghosts there were terrible liars.

I could see right through them.

It's rare that a defibrillator fails.

But when it does, no one is shocked.

I think my favorite word is drool.

It just rolls off the tongue.

This morning, I accidentally changed the GPS voice to a man's voice.

Now it says, "It's around here somewhere. Just keep driving."

I think I'm going to buy a dachshund.

A cowboy told me to get a long, little doggy.

I broke up with my girlfriend because I found out she was a communist.

I should have known. There were red flags everywhere.

My boss fired me, so I turned in my badge and gun.

Which opened a whole other can of worms since I'm only a janitor.

My daughter asked me why seagulls fly over the sea.

Because if they flew over the bay, they'd be baygulls.

I've always had a lot of respect for fishermen.

Now those are reel men.

I used to like The Picture of Dorian Gray.

But it gets old really fast.

I used to be in a music group called Cellophane.

We mostly wrapped.

I made a belt out of watches once.

It was a waist of time.

My packages were delivered, but all the goods were damaged during transport.

Now they are bads.

My friend has been depressed ever since he lost his feet in a mower accident.

He's never felt more de-feeted.

A Vatican priest tried to buy something from me over the internet.

But I don't take Papal.

Never, ever spell "part" backwards.

It's a trap!

"I'm sorry" and "I apologize" mean the same thing.

Except when you're at a funeral.

After we climbed the rise, my wife asked if I would color her hair.

But I wasn't willing to dye on that hill.

My inflatable house got a puncture last night.

Now I'm living in a flat.

I want to tell you about a girl who only eats plants.

You've probably never heard of herbivore.

I can cut a piece of wood in half just by looking at it.

I saw it with my own eyes.

I refuse to take my kid to see a child psychologist.

I don't think children should be psychologists.

I think yogurt must be a snack for smart people.

The package even says that it's cultured.

I love me a good hotel.

My wife got angry at me for kicking the dropped ice cubes under the refrigerator.

But now it's all just water under the fridge.

I'm reading a book about the history of glue.

I can't seem to put it down.

I love me a good hotel.

But I'm not ready to Marriott.

My friend and I had an argument about which vowel is the most important.

I won.

I threw a blanket over my son's train set when I heard my wife coming.

I think I managed to cover my tracks.

I don't think Alexander the Great was all he was cracked up to be.

I'd have called him, Alexander the Meh.

I love to write, but I make a lot of mistakes.

I think I have a Typo personality.

I always write my name in cursive.

It's my signature move.

For Valentine's Day, I decided to buy my wife some beads for her abacus.

It's the little things that count.

A waiter asked if I wanna box for my leftovers.

I told him I don't box, but I'd wrestle him for them.

My poet friend writes poetry that's not all that good.

But it could be verse.

I knew I shouldn't steal a mixer from the department store.

But it was a whisk I was willing to take.

Yesterday I gave my dad his 50th birthday card.

He looked at me and said, "You know, one would have been enough."

The world tongue-twister champion got arrested today.

I hear they're gonna give him a really tough sentence.

My son showed me how to record two television shows at the same time.

I didn't know it was remotely possible.

I'm thinking of putting all my money into raising cows with long legs.

But those are some high steaks.

Just so everyone's clear...

I'm going to put my glasses on.

Shout out to the man who invented the guillotine.

He knew how to get a head in life.

My wife and I laugh about how competitive we are.

But I laugh more.

Last week, someone slapped me at high frequency.

It still megahertz

When I'm sad, I like to make pork roast.

That way, I have a shoulder to cry on.

My son bought shoes for his frog.

They're open-toad.

My wife left me because I didn't do enough chores around the house.

I didn't do anything to deserve this.

For Halloween, I walked down the street dressed as a screwdriver.

I turned a few heads.

I couldn't connect my phone to Bluetooth, so I changed my password to Titanic.

Now it's synching.

I was sitting in traffic the other day.

That's probably why I got run over.

I like to give refrigerators to my friends as gifts.

Then I get to watch their faces light up when they open it.

My wife was depressed because she thought she looked fat, so she asked me to compliment her.

I told her that her eyesight is perfect.

I made a graph of all my past relationships.

There was an ex-axis and a why-axis.

My dentist asked me when was the last time I flossed.

I said, "You don't remember? You were right there."

The cashier asked me if I'd like the milk in a bag.

I told her to just leave it in the carton.

Last night my wife asked me, "Is it just me, or is the cat overweight."

Apparently, "It's just you" wasn't the right answer.

I don't trust art classes.

They're all a little too sketchy to me.

I just had an interview to see if I'm a good candidate for a nose job.

I think I blew it.

My son asked if I could put his shoes on.

I told him I didn't think they would fit me.

My wife threatened to divorce me is I gave our daughter a silly name.

I called her Bluff.

Everyone was on edge when our campsite was visited by Bigfoot.

It got in tents.

Managing your weight around the holidays just requires a little planning.

For example, I plan to take the batteries out of the scale on Wednesday.

To the person who stole my copy of Microsoft Office...

I will find you. You have my Word.

I wrote a research paper about the Bible.

There was a lot of cross referencing.

Never get food poisoning from Greek cheese.

It's a Feta worse than death.

I used to be against organ transplants.

But then I had a change of heart.

I heard Shakespeare had a cat, but I don't know what kind.

Tabby, or not tabby.

I complimented the steam roller driver for doing a good job.

He was flattered.

⌣

Last night I asked Siri why I'm so bad with women.

She said, "This is Alexa, idiot."

⌣

I thought my wife was joking when she told me to stop singing a Monkee's song.

Then I saw her face. Now I'm a believer.

⌣

I quit my job as a bartender for the mob.

It was a whiskey business.

You know, not everyone thinks of Cleopatra as beautiful.

But that's how Julius Caesar.

I saw a self-help book that claimed it could help me solve 50% of my problems.

So, I bought two books.

My wife told me she wants me to stop acting Canadian.

I have no idea what she's talking aboot.

I always wear my swim trunks under my pants when I go to work.

In case I decide to carpool.

We have a cow with a twitch.

We're going to use her to make beef jerky.

🥸

I accidentally used dog shampoo today.

Now I feel like such a good boy.

🥸

When I was eight I wanted a puppy, but my dad got me a log instead.

Sounds mean, but he was a wood boy.

🥸

I've been prescribed anti-gloating cream.

I can't wait to rub it in.

I got fired from the flower shop.

Apparently, I took too many leaves.

I finally cut ties with someone who was dragging me down.

Mountain climbing with a friend is hard.

I have a duck that doesn't handle dramatic situations very well.

It quacks under the pressure.

When I worked at the bookstore, someone asked me where the self-help section was.

I didn't tell them. That would defeat the purpose.

I've been trying to come up with jokes about airplanes.

But so far, none of them had landed correctly.

My new slacks have five leg holes.

They fit me like a glove.

My scarecrow won an award at the harvest festival.

He was outstanding in his field.

Not to brag, but I finished the jigsaw puzzle in six months.

The side of the box said 3-5 years.

I'm thinking of becoming a Jehovah's Witness.

I can see it opening a lot of doors for me.

I just don't know if I can trust subtraction.

Something about it doesn't add up.

My daughter's English professor was sent to prison.

He got a full sentence.

The store sold out quickly of the new Lego set my son wants.

People were lined up for blocks.

I've opened three birthday cards, and got $75!

On the other hand, I was fired from my job as a postman.

My neighbor and I share the same water supply.

We got a long well.

When I go golfing, I always carry two pairs of pants.

Never know when I'll get a hole in one.

One of the best channels on TV is all about origami.

Of course, it's paper view.

I created a gaming console completely by accident.

I'm calling it the Un-intendo.

I was thinking about the herb garden I had as a kid.

Good thymes.

I told a joke on a Zoom meeting and no one laughed.

It turns out I'm not remotely funny.

Someone stole my mood ring yesterday.

I don't know how I feel about it.

The only jokes I know about chemistry are all bad.

All the good ones argon.

A friend of mine thought about getting married, but decided to remain a bachelor.

So he is footloose and fiancèe-free.

Someone sawed the top off of a pyramid.

I think it's pointless.

I didn't have any money, so I had to pay my bookie with grape juice.

It's the first time I've ever Welched on a bet.

I didn't think pretending to be a pirate would be addicting.

But I'm hooked.

Thirty percent of pet owners let their pets sleep in their beds.

I tried it once. My goldfish died.

I lost my job as a mechanic.

They said I lacked fine motor skills.

There's one big difference between men and women.

When a woman says, "Smell this," it usually smells nice.

I have a bunch of jokes about unemployed people.

Unfortunately, none of them seem to work.

Dogs can't operate MRI machines.

But catscan.

I got hit in the head with a can of soda.

Luckily, it was a soft drink.

I think the mountains must be non-binary.

Someone told me there was gold in them/their hills.

I'm usually not superstitious.

But I am a little stitious.

My wife and I got into an argument about past, present, and future.

The argument was in tense.

I knew a librarian who had a tax-free side hustle.

It was completely off the books.

Archeologists have discovered what is believed to be the world's oldest bed sheet.

I'll update you as the story unfolds.

There was a kidnapping at the school today.

It's okay now. He woke up.

When I told my wife our neighbor died, she said, "Who? Ray?"

I thought it was a little too soon to celebrate.

I saw an idiot running on the treadmill at the gym this morning.

He put his water bottle in the Pringles holder.

I went to the salon, and there was hair all over the floor. Then I went to the mechanic, and there was oil all over the floor.

I can't wait to go to the bank.

This morning I tried to search for shellfish on the beach.

I stopped when I pulled a mussel.

I was wondering why the football was getting bigger.

Then it hit me.

I'm getting really sick of millenials attitudes lately.

Walking around like they rent the place.

I believe all witches should wear name tags.

Because right now, I can't tell witch is which.

To all the people out there suffering from paranoia, remember...

...you're not alone.

I just watched a documentary about beavers.

It was the best dam movie I've ever seen.

A friend of mine asked, "Bro, can you pass me that leaflet?"

I said, "Bro, chure."

Three years ago, I asked my crush to go out with me. Fast forward to last week, and I asked her to marry me.

She said no both times.

The clothes keep falling off the mannequins at the clothing store.

Someone needs to redress the problem.

I'm working on a new joke, but it's not matured yet.

I'm gonna wait until it's full groan.

My chiropractor always plays the same music on his speaker system.

He prefers hip-pop.

My wife got mad at me for being lazy.

It's not like I did anything.

The cross-eyed teacher got in trouble.

She couldn't control her pupils.

I wanted to tell a joke to someone with a broken hearing aid.

But he wouldn't hear of it.

My boss told me to attach two pieces of wood together.

I totally nailed it.

My wife fainted on the airport's baggage carousel.

Eventually, she came around.

I bought my wife a matching belt and bag for her birthday.

We'll have that vacuum cleaner working again in no time.

They finally caught the two theives who stole a calendar.

They each got six months.

The hotdog vendor didn't get his license renewed.

Guess he didn't pass the mustard.

I found a great place to order sausages.

I'll send you a link.

My wife has a really hard time getting to sleep.

But I can do it with my eyes closed.

I'm thinking of getting braces.

Just as a stop-gap measure.

Someone ripped the fifth page out of my calendar.

I'm dismayed.

My dad fell through the ice once.

By the time we got to him, he was a pop-sicle.

My wife is divorcing me because she says I think I know more than she does about everything.

I said, "But let me explain."

All the toilets were stolen from the police station.

The cops still have nothing to go on.

I told my wife she should embrace her mistakes.

So she gave me a hug.

I'm giving away all my dead batteries.

They are free of charge.

The man who invented the knock-knock joke was recently honored.

He won the no-bell prize.

By law, you have to turn on your headlights when it's raining in Sweden.

How am I supposed to know when it's raining in Sweden?

My wife broke her finger today.

But on the other hand, she is completely fine.

My son just threw a milk carton at me.

How dairy!

A lot of Presidents are guilty of something. But not Abraham Lincoln.

He was in a cent.

I found out last night my toaster wasn't waterproof.

I was shocked.

When I'm hungry, I like to eat bulbs.

It's a light snack.

If you get a job as an executioner, always use an axe.

It's easier to get a head.

Atoms are untrustworthy.

They make up everything!

It took awhile for me to master Braille.

People asked me if I play soccer for money.

But I just do it for the kicks.

It took awhile for me to master Braille.

But eventually, I got a feel for it.

I'm trying to remember what the French word for white is.

But my mind keeps going blanc.

My girlfriend broke up with me when she found out I only had nine toes.

She was lack toes intolerant.

I laugh every time I see mountains.

They're hill areas.

At the zoo, my son asked me why the flamingos lift up one leg.

Well, duh. If they lifted both legs, they would fall over.

I have a disease where I can't stop telling airport jokes.

The doctor says it's terminal.

I once dreamed I was floating in an ocean of orange soda.

Actually, it was more of a Fanta sea.

My irrational phobia of German sausages has not gotten any better.

I fear the wurst!

My bicycle won't stand up on its own.

I think it's two-tired.

I accidentally ate aluminum foil.

I'm going to sheet metal.

My aunt went to the doctor because her eyes are bothering her.

He gave her some aunt-eye-biotics.

My daughter asked me how to get a blind person to see.

I assume on a boat.

A virus is making people forget 80s rock bands.

Nobody knows The Cure.

I have a pretty good joke about ropes.

But I'm gonna skip it.

The invisible man turned down a job offer.

It was something he couldn't see himself doing.

﹩

Bigfoot is sometimes confused with Sasquatch.

Yeti never complains.

﹩

I don't trust big cats.

Sometimes they're lion. Other times, they're cheetahs.

﹩

I used to be a fisherman.

But I got caught playing hooky.

I keep trying to lose weight.

But it keeps finding me.

I tried blindfolded archery for the first time yesterday..

I didn't know what I was missing.

I'm glad Spring is finally here!

I'm so excited, I wet my plants.

At the age of 65, my grandmother started walking 10 miles a day.

Now, twenty years later, we have no idea where she is.

I usually charge money for my dad jokes about roofs.

But the first one is on the house.

I just found out my friend has a secret life as a priest.

It's his altar ego.

My landscaper keeps giving me investment advice.

But I just don't know about hedge funds.

I turned down a job where I'd be paid in vegetables.

The celery was just unacceptable.

I really like my new shampoo.

It's head and shoulders above the others.

Our local post office burned down yesterday.

I think it's a case of black mail.

When your husband says he will do something, he will do it.

You don't have to remind him every other month.

I daughter cried when I took her to "Take Your Kid to Work Day."

She looked around the office and said, "Where are all the clowns you said you work with?"

There's a guy on my bowling team who is always late.

He has no time to spare.

My mother said, "One man's trash is another man's treasure."

Turns out I'm adopted.

A genie granted me one wish, and I said, "I wish I were you."

The genue saud, "Weurd, but alrught."

I have a neighbor who counts like, "1, 3, 5, 7, 9..."

I find that odd.

I quit my job at the helium factory.

I won't be spoken to in that tone.

I asked my friend what it's like to live in China.

He said he can't complain.

I told my boss I was going to the bathroom, but I didn't specify which one.

I went home.

I wanted to go trick-or-treating in my skeleton costume.

But I had no body to go with.

Singing in the shower is fun until you get shampoo in your mouth.

Then it's a soap opera.

When asked to rate my listening skills, my wife said, "You're an eight out on a scale to ten."

I have no idea why she wants me to urinate on a skeleton.

My old girlfriend once accused me of invading her privacy.

She didn't say it to my face, but I read it in her diary.

I've heard Oslo is a particularly dangerous city.

There's Norway I'd ever go there.

Everyone was mad at me because I overcooked the T-bone last night.

We all make miss-steaks.

My wife asked me from the other room if I ever felt like someone was stabbing a voodoo doll that looked like me.

I said, I didn't. She said, "How about now?"

Our librarian is way too strict.

She always goes by the books.

The archaeological team uncovered the remains of an undercooked steak at their latest excavation.

It was a rare find.

That's the tenth passenger today who's called me a terrible bus driver.

I don't know where these people get off!

My mother was shorter than most.

She was a minimum.

One of my favorite local bands is 999MB.

But they haven't gotten a gig yet.

My wife said she wants to pursue her dream of learning to drive a steamroller.

I said I'm not going to stand in her way.

Banks should do a better job keeping money in their ATMs.

I went to five today, and none of them could give me cash due to insufficient funds.

When I was an attorney, I had a lot of wrongful convictions.

Being a lawyer is just trial and error.

I bought shoes from a drug dealer once.

I don't know what he laced them with, but I was tripping all day.

My wife is mad at me because I never buy her flowers.

I honestly didn't know she sold flowers.

I couldn't go into the diner because the sign on the door said, "Shoes must be worn."

Unfortunately, my shoes were brand new.

I collect rocks, and I once found a rock that was 1,760 yards long.

It was quite the milestone.

The doctor told me I'm going deaf.

The news was hard to hear.

My boss just told me to dress for the job I want, not for the job I have.

So tomorrow I'm going as Peter Pan.

I'm reading a book about ship building.

It's riveting.

An invisible man married an invisible woman.

Their kids were nothing to look at either.

I got laid off from the candle factory.

Business tapered off after the holidays.

I once fell in love with the person next door.

It was a lawn-distance relationship.

People in Greece absolutely hate waking up at dawn.

Dawn is tough on Greece.

My cow tried to jump the barbed wire fence.

It led to udder destruction.

I heard that Tweety Bird retired and moved to the Bahamas.

Livin' the dweam.

My daughter wants to dress up as a rodent for Halloween.

I told her to gopher it.

My wife threatened to leave me for putting on different clothes every hour.

I told her, "Wait. I can change."

A cop pulled me over and asked, "How high are you?"

I said, "No, sir. It's 'hi, how are you?'"

I asked a friend for a good name for a dinosaur, and he said, "Triceratops."

I don't take advice from him anymore. Sara Topps is a terrible name for a dinosaur.

I spent my life savings on pasta.

It was worth every penne.

My wife told me a little person who escaped prison by climbing down the wall on a rope.

I said, "Honey, that's a little con descending, don't you think?"

Someone keeps stealing carrots from my garden.

I'm going to get down to the root of the problem.

I thought about divorcing my wife, but I don't want to pay the alimony.

That's the high cost of leaving.

I have a Swedish friend who doesn't like modern music.

He was Bjorn in the wrong generation.

There's one major difference between me and a calendar.

A calendar has dates.

My friend was explaining electricity to me.

I was like, "Watt!!"

My wife told me to stop being an idiot and just be myself.

I told her she needed to make up her mind.

A drunk man walked into a bar...

...then a table... then a chair.

I'm having a hard time getting the yoga instructor to leave my house.

Every time I tell him to leave, he says, "Namaste."

My trainer balked when I told him I only wanted to work out one side of my body.

But I'm exercising my rights.

I quite my job as a postman when they handed me the first letter to deliver.

It just wasn't for me.

There's a rumor going around about butter.

But I'm not going to spread it.

My wife asked me if glass coffins will ever become popular.

Remains to be seen.

I scared my cab driver when I talked to him from the backseat.

Apparently, he's been driving hearses for the last 25 years.

I wasn't surprised when the price of books went up.

There's always inflation in that business.

A short fortune teller escaped from prison.

Now there's a small medium at large.

I have a friend who hates living in the Central U.S.

She's in a constant state of Missouri.

I told my doctor that I think I'm being followed by squirrels.

He said I must be nuts.

I accidentally swallowed a bunch of Scrabble tiles.

My next trip to the bathroom could spell disaster.

When I work out, I don't mind leg day.

It's the two days after I can't stand.

I found my wife checking out our marriage certificate.

Turns out she was looking for the expiration date.

I want to be cremated.

It will be my last chance to have a smokin' hot body.

The lifeguard was unable to save the hippie.

He was too far out, man.

The gambling addiction hotline is a popular phone number.

They say that every fifth caller is a winner.

I've gotten to the age where I no longer want to party like it's 1999.

I want to grocery shop like it's 1999.

I'm proud to say that yesterday I wore something from when I was in college, and it still fit.

It was a pair of socks, but still.

I have a friend who is a poet, and he went bankrupt.

He odes everyone.

I didn't get the job because I didn't fill out the contact information on the application.

But I thought the glasses made it clear that I don't have contacts.

Little people have a poor sense of humor.

Most of the jokes are over their heads.

My kids insulted me this morning while I was
drinking coffee.

It was just a light roast.

I told the surgeon I would save money by sewing
myself up.

He said, "Suture self."

My son asked me if French fries were made in
France.

I told him I'd heard they were made in Greece.

The store is having a sell on tennis balls.

It's first come, first serve.

My neighbors always listern to great music.

Someone told me an earthquake joke the other day.

It cracked me up.

My neighbors always listern to great music.

Whether they like it or not.

I'm thinking of taking my banana to the doctor.

It's not peeling well.

Some of my warts are from viruses, but others are from stress.

Those are my worry warts.

I believe that beer is my enemy.

Luckily, God says to love your enemy.

Someone stole my identity last week.

They sent it back with $100 and a note that said, "So sorry. I hope everything works out."

I have a friend who is obsessed with monorails, and that's all she wants to talk about.

She has a one-track mind.

I gave up smoking and drinking.

That was the worst 15 minutes of my life.

I ate a kid's meal at McDonald's today.

His mother was not happy.

My daughter asked me why celebrities are always so cool.

It's because of all the fans they have.

A limbo player walked into a bar.

He was disqualified.

My son asked me if we're pyromaniacs.

I said, "We arson."

I went to a restaurant on the moon.

Great food, no atmosphere.

Somebody told me a joke about paper.

It was tearable.

The dentist and the manicurist got divorced.

They fought tooth and nail.

I named my puppy after my ex-wife.

Passive-Aggressive Psycho is finally potty-trained.

My wife is mad because her jigsaw puzzle is missing one of its 5,000 pieces.

But that's nothing. My puzzle is missing 4.999 pieces.

A friend said the top of my head looks like a plateau.

That's the highest form of flattery.

I spent days trying to fix the GPS.

But I was getting nowhere.

At the slaughterhouse, I slipped on a piece of liver and fell into a vat of cow intestines.

It was offal.

My son told me he would call me later.

I told him to just call me dad.

I had a paintball exam once.

I passed with flying colors.

The restaurant I go to makes salads that are a little on the dry side.

It's definitely something that needs a dressing.

I've finally been cured of my compulsive buying of boats.

Those antibuyyachtics certainly did the trick.

Anytime my kids are cold I tell them to go stand in the corner.

It's always 90 degrees there.

All I do at work all day is crush cans.

It's soda pressing.

My kids are upset because I put pepper in the soup.

They really loved that cat.

Someone asked me if I wanted to read a book about 1980's hairstyles.

I'm gonna mullet over.

Someone gave me some German currency, but I think it's counterfeit.

I have question marks.

My son asked me, "What's a Grecian urn?"

I told him that depended on what he did for a living.

A friend of mine was married by a shotgun wedding.

It was a matter of wife or death.

I heard Charlie Brown quit his job.

He's tired of working for Peanuts.

My laptop was destroyed when someone spilled apple juice on it.

It was a cider attack.

I've decided I'm going to apply for a job at the diner.

I think I can bring a lot to the table.

When I came home, my wife told me the baby had been crying for hours and asked if I could take over.

So, I cried for hours.

Free legless parrot.

No perches necessary.

I know a guy who writes songs about sewing machines.

He's a Singer-Songwriter. Or sew it seams.

They caught the guy who stole the calendar from the office.

He got twelve months.

When we were canoeing, my wife asked if I'd like to use this paddle or the other one.

I said, "Either/oar."

I've never told my wife that she cooks well.

But she keeps cooking anyway.

I refuse to eat clownfish.

They taste a little funny.

I used to be a plumber, but I couldn't do it anymore.

It was hard watching my life's work go down the drain.

I have a cousin who grew up near Chernobyl.

He can count on three hands how often his family has visited him there.

I got hired today after I told the interviewer I'd gone to Yale.

I really needed this new yob.

The best present I ever received was a broken drum.

You just can't beat that!

My friend told me that for someone with a Bachelors, a Masters, and a PhD, I'm not very smart.

It was a third-degree burn.

I really can't stand Orion's belt.

It's a big waist of space.

I think the cashier at the store is into me.

She was definitely checking me out.

My therapist told me I have trouble expressing my emotions.

I can't say I'm surprised.

When I was in school, we had to assemble a skeleton, and I hid one of the arm bones as a joke.

No one found that humerus.

My grandpa always said, "Fight fire with fire."

Great man. Terrible firefighter.

A woman wants me to take her to dinner, but I don't do that with married women.

She's my wife, but I make no exceptions.

People are usually shocked to find out I have a police record.

But I love all their greatest hits.

My wife gave me one last chance to get over my addiction of using a whistle around the house.

Unfortunately, I blew it.

I try to pay proper respect to garden fences.

They're often overlooked.

My kid is passed out on the floor because he threatened to hold his breathe until I gave him ice cream.

Well, I don't negotiate with terrorists.

Everyone laughed when I said I wanted to be a comedian.

Well, no one's laughing now.

My ex-wife asked me why we needed walkie-talkies if our relationship is over.

I said, "Our relationship is what? Over."

My boss said he was going to fire whoever has the worst posture.

I have a hunch it will be me.

I have an onion that likes to rhyme.

It's a rapscallion.

The electrician had been in the hospital, and he's not getting any better.

The doctors are going to pull the plug on him.

Whoever created the shovel deserves more credit.

It was a groundbreaking invention.

My therapist told me I have a difficult time picking up on social clues.

I think she must be in love with me.

The cable repair man asked me what time it was.

I told him it was between 8 am and 1 pm.

My boss asked me why I was wearing one black sock and one white sock.

I told him I have another pair just like it at home.

I cried like a baby when the policeman gave me a ticket.

It was a moving violation.

In high school, I couldn't wait to become a senior.

Now, I'm not really looking forward to it.

I just found out Albert Einstein was a real person.

All this time I thought he was a theoretical physicist.

My tent got stolen from my campsite, so I went to the insurance agency.

Turns out, I wasn't covered.

I used to work at a factory that made decent products.

It was a satis-factory.

I love putting on warm underwear fresh out of the dryer.

In a related story, I've been banned from the laudromat.

My bearded dragon has five legs.

He has a reptile dysfunction.

I called my landlord to tell him I got a leak in the sink.

He said, "Well, when you gotta go, you gotta go."

I was told crocodiles can grow up to 15 feet.

But most of them only have four.

I always misspell the word "subtle."

Because the "b" is...well, you know.

I recently saw a man and a woman wrapped in a barcode.

They must have been an item.

I couldn't remember how to throw a boomerang.

But then it came back to me.

The divorce attorney has a really good deal going.

Your satisfaction is guaranteed or your honey back.

I worked so hard, the police arrested me.

They charged me with resisting a rest.

A friend of mine sells unpasteurized milk on the black market.

He's been accused of skimming.

My ex-girlfriend asked me why she always looks bad in pictures.

And answering that question is why she's my EX-girlfriend.

Scuba divers always fall backwards out of the boat.

If they fell forward, they'd still be in the boat.

I went to the funeral of my dentist yesterday.

I guess he's filled his last cavity.

If you think English is easy to learn...

...just realize, every "C" in "Pacific Ocean" is pronounced differently.

I was on the toilet when I realized I was going to be late for work.

I thought, "I don't have time for this crap."

People in Dubai don't like the Flintstones.

But the people in Abu Dhabi do.

I lost 20% of my couch.

Ouch!

I asked a lady at the bar if she was looking for the best night of her life, and she said, "No!"

I think I have a chance!

I will be telling jokes telepathically today.

So if you think of something funny, that was me.

My therapist told me to stop making up scenarios in my head.

Which is weird, because I don't even have a therapist.

My daughter wants to invent a pencil with an eraser on both ends.

It's pointless, if you ask me.

A lot of women say their husbands never listen to them.

I'm proud to say I've never heard my wife say that.

Getting stung by eight bees can kill you, but add one more bee, and you're safe.

That's because it's bee 9.

My sister keeps applying to the post office, but she'll never get hired.

It's a mail-dominated industry.

People keep stealing ladders from the hardware store.

Further steps need to be taken.

My son asked if I could tell him what a solar eclipse is.

I said, "No, sun."

My my

I asked the sandwich maker if I could get a turkey on rye with pickles.

He said that they only accept cash or card.

My my

My girlfriend poked me in the eyes.

I stopped seeing her for a while.

My my

Before I die, I'm going to eat a whole bag of unpopped popcorn.

That should make the cremation a lot more interesting.

I just bought a pub.

I paid a little more than I wanted, but it's still a bar gain.

My wife seems to think she is running the show in our family.

And once I've completed this long to-do list she told me I'd better have finished by the end of the day, I'm going to set her straight.

I tried washing my car with my son.

Next time I'm going to use a sponge instead.

I think I have bad posture.

But it's just a hunch.

It's time I finally share some jokes about library books.

They are long overdue.

My wife made reservations for a holiday cruise.

I guess that means we're going to Easter Island.

I really enjoy eating a good hot dog.

I relish every bit.

Never date a tennis player.

Love means nothing to them.

I lost my job as a mime.

Must have been something I said.

People ask me all the time if I'm an optimist.

I certainly hope so.

The good news it, my phone fell down a flight of stairs, but it's not broken.

The bad news is, it was in my pocket at the time.

Someone broke into my house last night and stole all of my fruit.

I'm peachless.

I took my daughter to the doctor after she was hurt in a pillow fight.

She has a concushion.

I recently visited the world's tiniest wind turbine exhibit.

Honestly...not a big fan.

Never, ever buy flowers from a monk.

Only you can prevent florist friars.

I was on a paleontology dig the other day, and I thought I found a dinosaur's ulna.

It was a fossil arm.

My friend who is a drummer is coming out of retirement.

There will be repercussions.

My wife asked, "Why do you keep pushing all my buttons?"

I said, "I'm looking for the mute button."

My landlord tells me that he feels inadequate lately.

I wonder if he has a complex.

My wife said, "You have no sense of direction, do you?"

I said, "Where did that come from?"

I regret buying that straight jacket.

I thought I would look good, but I couldn't pull it off.

Yesterday, I accidentally swallowed some food coloring.

The doctor says I'm okay, but I feel like I dyed a little.

Not to brag, but I made six figures last year.

Coincidentally, I was also named worst employee at the toy factory.

I stopped asking my wife where she wants to eat.

Now I ask, "Guess where I'm taking you." And whatever she says is where we go.

I've gotten really good at stealing cigarette lighters using sleight of hand.

I've got some Bics up my sleeve.

The Indian restaurant made me sign a contract saying I wouldn't share their flatbread recipe.

Just their standard naan disclosure agreement.

Have you ever heard of the blind cyclops brothers?

Neither have eye.

I always bring a ruler to bed.

I like to know how long I've slept.

My friend showed me a picture of a horse-drawn carriage.

There's no way a horse drew that carriage.

People tell me I fixate on the pain in my bad tooth.

I'm abscessed by it.

I owe my whole life to sidewalks.

They've been keeping me off the streets for years.

My dad always said, "Don't be quick to find faults."
He was a great man.

A terrible geologist, but a great man.

I'm kinda nervous about this skydiving instructor my wife has befriended.

I think she fell for him.

〰️👨

I've worked for 24 hours straight.

I'm gonna call it a day.

〰️👨

My wife was drunk and watching a movie and yelling at the TV, "Don't go in there! Don't go into the church, you moron!"

She gets like this when she watches our old wedding video.

〰️👨

Once, a genie granted me one wish, and I wished I was rich.

Now my name is Rich.

My son broke his arm in two places.

We don't let him go to those places anymore.

Yesterday I managed to touch my toes.

It was quite a stretch for me.

I read recently that 3 out of every 10 people have a fear of hurdles.

Most will never get over it.

A friend's always come to me with their issues.

So I'm canceling my subscriptions.

I remember every tree I ever cut down when I was a lumberjack.

I kept a log.

I don't know why people tell me I have no willpower.

I've quit smoking many times.

My son is mad at me because we left the trampoline park early.

But he's the one who told me he was ready to bounce.

I used to own a company that drilled for oil.

I drove it into the ground.

I got a job as a flight attendant.

I think I'm gonna be going places.

I can't remember the name of my homing pigeon.

But it'll come to me.

I left the pot boiling too long and all the water boiled away.

It will be mist.

People say gravity is important, but if you remove it...

...you get gravy.

I'm glad I sold my submarine stocks when I did.

That industry has really taken a dive.

I've written a book on penguins.

Looking back, paper would have probably been more efficient.

My computer was cold because I didn't turn it off before I went to bed.

Turns out, I left the Windows open.

My friend Tony said he would appreciate it if I wouldn't say his name backwards.

I asked, "Y not?"

I meditated today.

The judge called it premeditated, but whatever.

Shakespeare never wrote a work about puns.

It would have been a play on words.

My teenage son treats me like a god.

He acts like I don't exist until he wants something.

I woke up to find my credit card laying on top of my keyboard.

I can't wait to see what drunk me bought sober me.

My daughter is worried about the full moon.

It's just a phase.

My friend's four-year-old had been learning Spanish and still doesn't know how to say please.

I think that's poor for four.

I failed my calculus exam because I was seated with an identical twin on either side of me.

I couldn't differentiate between them.

I went to a bar last night called Pillar of Salt.

Looking back, it was a mistake.

I told my doctor I think I have hearing problems, and he asked me to describe the symptoms.

I told him that Homer is a fat slob and his wife Marge has blue hair.

When I was six, I asked my dad if we were Scottish.

He told me to shut up and finish my whiskey.

Americans can't switch from pounds to kilograms overnight.

That would cause mass confusion.

They told me I was fired because my communication skills were not good enough.

I didn't know what to say.

A man at the Indian restaurant choked to death on his naan.

The police are investigating it as a hummucide.

I just found out Yoda has a last name.

It's Layheehoo.

A swarm of flying insects is threatening our town.

The government is deploying the swat team.

Our neighbor was up all night digging three holes.

Well, well, well.

Everyone thinks I'm tight with money.

But I'm not buying it.

I don't always whoop.

But when I do, there it is.

At first, I didn't think my chiropractor was very good at his job.

Now I stand corrected.

My church has been having a severe pest control problem lately.

Let us spray.

At the monastery, I saw a man in the kitchen making chips.

I don't know if he was a fryer or a chip monk.

When I told my wife I alphabetized her spices, she asked me, "How do you find the time?"

I said, "It's right there, next to the Tarragon."

I heard that the bread factory burned down.

That business is toast.

We do not throw away perfect good food in my household.

We put it in a plastic container, wait for it to go bad, then throw it away.

Someone stole my limbo stick.

I mean, how low can you go?

I finished reading The Hunchback of Notre Dame, and I loved it.

I just love a protagonist with a twisted-back story.

I used to work at a Chinese export business.

But I got jaded.

I invented a measuring cup for the blind that tells them out loud how full it is.

It speaks volumes.

I always hide the liquor in my haunted house.

The spirits can't handle their boos.

My shirt made a loud boom when it fell to the floor.

Mainly because I was in it.

If you ever need a smoke while you're on a boat, but you don't have anything to light a cigarette, throw a cigarette overboard.

Then it will be a cigarette lighter.

The janitor was arrested yesterday.

He found out the hard way that grime doesn't pay.

Dieting isn't as hard as people think.

It's just mind over platter.

Ｗ

When life give you lemons, make lemonade.

But if life gives you melons, you're probably dyslexic.

Ｗ

I was driving to work, and robbers jumped in my car and stole everything.

They were pirates of the car I be in.

Ｗ

I'm practicing for a bug-eating contest.

I've got butterflies in my stomach.

My former girlfriend has gone through the process to become a female priest, but the Vatican isn't happy about it.

At least that's what my ex communicated.

My former girlfriend has gone through the process to become a female priest, but the Vatican isn't happy about it.

Someone keeps sending me flowers with the bulbs cut off.

I think I'm being stalked.

Some people worry that their smart phone or smart TV is spying on them.

But their vacuum has been gathering dirt on them for years.

I have a lot of jokes about water.

But I only do dry humor.

I bought a sports car made completely of wood.

It's a Lumberghini.

I accidentally drank holy water with my laxative.

I'm about to start a religious movement.

I just joined a dating site for arsonists.

So far, I have a lot of matches.

I have an inferiority complex.

But, it's not a very good one.

My wife doesn't think I can get rich by eating.

Apparently, she's never heard of fortune cookies.

After hiking through the woods, I tested positive for Lyme disease.

That really ticks me off.

It's true when they say music can transport you to another place.

A coffee shop was playing today's Top 40, so I went to another place.

The doctor said, "You can see the new baby, but your wife didn't make it."

I said, "Well, can you show me the baby she did make?"

My wife accused me of stealing her thesaurus.

Not only was I shocked. I was appalled, aghast, and dismayed.

My first job was working at an orange juice factory.

But I got canned because I couldn't concentrate.

I'm going to take a hot shower.

It's like a cold shower, but with me in it.

I have a condition so that every time I go to the library, I steal a book.

I should get that checked out.

I asked my wife a question while she was applying a mud pack.

You should have seen the filthy look she gave me.

﹩

I don't always like working as a coffee salesman.

But the job has its perks.

﹩

My horse will only come out of the stable after dark.

What a night mare.

﹩

I can't imagine haunted houses like storms.

The rain probably dampens their spirits.

My sister bet me $15 that I couldn't build a car out of spaghetti.

You should have seen her face when I drove pasta.

Anteaters are the healthiest of all animals.

Their stomachs are full of little anty-bodies.

Today, I broke the can opener.

Now it's a can't opener.

A firefighter told me my smoke detectors were too told.

I think he's just being an alarmist.

I used to be addicted to soap.

But I got clean.

I wish someone could tell me what oblivious means.

Because I have no idea.

My wife and I make pizza together, and her job is to shred the cheese.

She's the gratest.

I used to tell a chemistry joke all the time.

But it never gets a reaction.

I hate Russian Dolls.

They are so full of themselves.

I'm tired after doing five sets.

I was doing diddly squats.

I put a high-voltage electric fence around my property.

My neighbor is dead against it.

I had a happy childhood. My Dad used to put me in tires and roll me down hills.

Those were Goodyears.

I hung a copy of the U. S. Constitution on my wall.

It is the decoration of independence.

Every morning when I go for a walk, I get hit be the same bike.

It's a vicious cycle.

Poop jokes aren't my favorite kind of jokes.

But they're a solid number 2.

As a kid, my parents told me I could be anyone I wanted to be.

Turns out, identity theft is a crime.

I didn't enjoy my vacation in Germany.

There were so many people and the streets were too krauted.

I went to the postcard museum the other day.

Nothing to write home about.

And God said, "Come forth and receive eternal life."

But I came fifth and won a toaster.

An archaeologist friend of mine threw a party because he unearthed a dinosaur tibia.

It was quite the shin dig.

The electrician left work early today.

Business was light.

At first, I was excited about my new job as a hotel receptionist.

Then I started to have reservations.

Police haven't solved the convenience store beer theft.

It's a cold case.

I made chicken salad last night.

Apparently, they prefer grain.

I hate negative numbers.

And I'll stop at nothing to avoid them.

Once you've seen one guy attacked by a bear...

You've seen a maul.

I have a friend who always argues over which is better, wigwams or teepees.

That's just two tents for me.

The people next door just bought a horse.

He's our neigh-bor.

I only know 25 letters of the alphabet.

I don't know Y.

I went to the funeral of the inventor of anagrams.

It was real fun.

My wife told me that it was her fervent hope that I might be slapped.

She's so passive aggressive.

I know what a Freudian slip is.

It's when you say one thing, but mean your mother.

The police have no idea how the hackers managed to escape.

Best they can think is they just ransomware.

I learned to never play tennis with a cymbal.

It makes a terrible racket.

I took a urine test at the hospital the other day.

My kleptomania is getting out of hand.

A good burglar always keeps his eyes open for something they can steal.

They look for windows of opportunity.

I don't know if I have the best ceiling in the world.

But it's definitely up there.

My lion tamer friend went bankrupt, and they took almost everything.

But they couldn't take his pride.

My wife left me because I'm a compulsive gambler.

I'd do anything to win her back.

My parents raised me as an only child.

Which really angered my sister.

I heard of a guy who gets paid to sleep.

That would be my dream job.

Last Week, my dentist was doing half-price teeth cleanings.

It was a Plaque Friday event.

I recently wrote a book about onions.

Read it and weep!

I'd like to thank Merriam-Webster to teaching me the definition of plethora.

It really means a lot.

The doctor says I have high nitrates.

So I'm switching to day rates.

I got the ultimate compliment from my doctor during my last physical.

He said that I'm morbidly a beast.

I was raised from birth by a pack of hyenas.

Boy, did we have some laughs.

My doctor was taken aback when I saw him about a suspicious-looking mole.

Guess I should have just left it in the garden.

I won $3 million and donated a quarter of it to charity.

Now I have $2,999,999.75.

To the person who stole my glasses...

I will find you. I have contacts.

I don't know about this new chair lift.

It's driving me up the wall.

Last week, I took my hearing aid in for repair.

I've heard nothing since.

A hole was found in the wall to the women's locker room.

The police are looking into it.

My garden statue has an excellent sense of style.

It's a metro-gnome.

I opened a business weighing tiny objects.

It's a small scale operation.

Someday you'll find someone who will be obsessed with you.

It'll probably be a dog, but it is what it is.

My son asked me my opinion about global warming.

But I've never really thawed about it.

I asked a Frenchman if he has any gaming consoles.

He said, "Wii."

I wanted to ensure my wife woke up with a big smile on her face.

And that's why we don't have sharpies in the house anymore.

I went to the zoo, but all they had was one dog.

It was a shitzu.

I used to pray for a bicycle every Christmas, but never got one.

So I stole a bike, and then prayed for forgiveness.

I used to work at a stationary store.

But I didn't feel like I was going anywhere.

I think we missed an opportunity when we called them electricians.

They could have been power rangers.

Huge shout-out to those of us who danced next to the speakers at concerts in the 1980s.

No, seriously, please shout at us, because we are all deaf now.

I accidentally got my hand caught in the blender.

That's the last time I try to make a handshake.

I was going to say something rude about my friend's cow, but I held my tongue.

I don't want there to be any beef between us.

I don't need Google.

My wife knows everything.

I just found out the owner of the local hobby shop is a convict felon.

I'd always thought he was a model citizen.

I suppose I'd better clean out the fridge.

Something just closed it from the inside.

More from Xandland Press

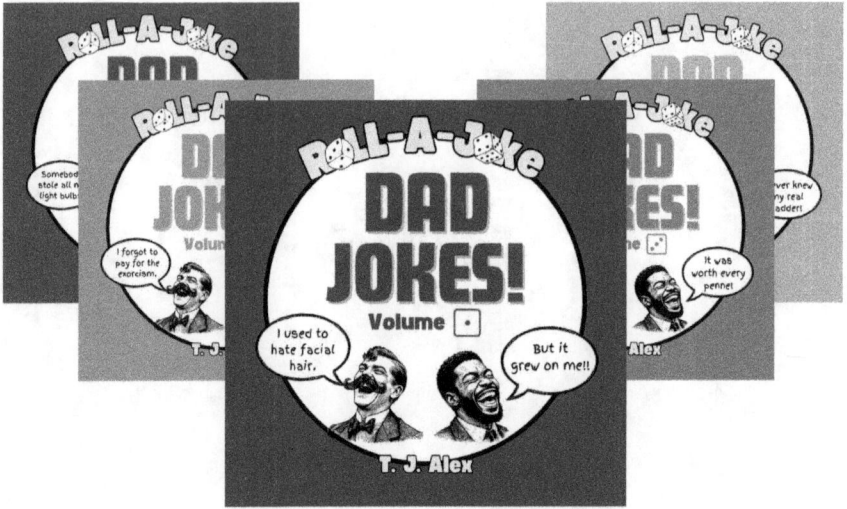

Roll-A-Joke Dad Joke books (6 Volumes):

Roll the dice to find out which Dad Joke
your kids will be subjected to!
Provides HOURS of fun and laughs (or groans)!

The Dead Fall series
by Joseph Xand:

Zombie novels that
have been compared
to Stephen King's
The Stand and
The Walking Dead.

Nosferatu:
A Symphony of Horror

A novelization of the classic
1922 film, written by Joseph
Xand and edited by T. J. Alex

www.ingramcontent.com/pod-product-compliance
Lightning Source LLC
LaVergne TN
LVHW051412080426
835508LV00022B/3040